Living *with* Healthy Relationships

By Judy Murphy

 GRASS ROOTS PRESS
Edmonton, Alberta

Living with Healthy Relationships is published by

Grass Roots Press
Phone: 1-780-413-6491
Fax: 1-780-413-6582
Web: www.grassrootsbooks.net

Author: Judy Murphy
Content consultation: Pam Algar, Registered Psychologist
Substantive editors: Pat Campbell and Linda Kita-Bradley
Clear language editor: Jo Petite
Copy editor: Deirdre Ah Shene
Consultant: Jenny Horsman
Illustrator: Val Lawton
Book design: Lara Minja, Lime Design Inc

We acknowledge the financial support of the Government of Canada through the Book Publishing Industry Development Program (BPIDP) for our publishing activities.

We acknowledge the support of the
Alberta Foundation for the Arts
for our publishing programs.

We acknowledge funding from the Adult Learning, Literacy and Essential Skills Program, Human Resources and Social Development Canada.

Library and Archives Canada Cataloguing in Publication

Murphy, Judy, 1942–
     Living with healthy relationships / written by Judy Murphy;
illustrated by Val Lawton.

Includes bibliographical references.
ISBN 978-1-926583-07-5

     1. Readers for new literates. 2. Interpersonal relations.
I. Lawton, Val, 1962– II. Title.

PE1126.N43M869 2009   428.6'2   C2008-906230-2

Printed in Canada

Table of Contents

• Thank You •

Many people helped to put this book together.

Five focus groups were organized in Alberta to share ideas and knowledge about the content and appearance of the books in the Easy-to-Read Health Series. I wish to give special thanks to participants in Alberta's literacy and community programs. Many people took part, and the following people gave permission to print their names

Amanda Akkerman
Ann
Bill Littlejohn
C. Kameyosit
C. Monias
Darrell Demeria
Dave A. Ramsden
Debbie Longo
Della Akkerman
Delia Manychief
Denise Banack
Dione Dubois
Elvis Quintal
Ernie Lonewolf
Fred Cazon
Glen Dumont

Gloria Herbert
Hazel
Helen
Iwalani A. Post
Ive
Jeanne Longo
Jim Judd
John A. Butler
Jung Zheng
Kathy Helms
L. Miskenack
Lynne Gendron
Lynne W.
Liz
Mark Garbutt
Marvin Mochid
Matthew Ivan
Mavis Prevost
Monica Catellier
Nora Potts
Priscilla Wallin
Rachel Kretz
Robert Desjarlais
Shawn Worbs
Sherien Lo
Susan Murray

I thank those who facilitated the focus groups and the programs and agencies that hosted them: Dani Ducross, Coordinator, Adult Literacy Program in Lacombe; Anna Reitman, Principal, Edmonton John Howard Society's Alternative Learning Program; Berniece Gowan and Sandra Loschnig, focus group facilitators, Calgary Elizabeth Fry Society; and Vesna Kavaz, Coordinator, Words Work in Athabasca.

People participating in community-based learning programs in the following organizations told me what information they would like to see in *Living with Healthy Relationships*: Edmonton John Howard Society, Elizabeth Fry Society of Edmonton, and The Learning Centre Literacy Association. I thank these people for their interest and for freely sharing their ideas.

Participants in Edmonton John Howard's Adult Transitional Learning Centre (ATLC), Elizabeth Fry Society of Edmonton, and The Learning Centre Literacy Association wrote stories about healthy relationships. I thank Debbie Lanthlin, K. Steele, and Maggie M.

The executive staff members at Boyle McCauley Health Centre, hosts of the Easy-to-Read Health Series project, have been enthusiastic and avid supporters. I thank Cecilia Blasetti, Colleen Novotny, and Wendy Kalamar.

The project has been guided by an Advisory Committee. Each member has given her time and knowledge to guide this project. I thank Marg Budd, Tobacco Reduction Consultant, Capital Health; Pat Campbell, President of Grass Roots Press; Ann Goldblatt, Project Evaluator; Maggie Mercredi, Coordinator, Changing Paths and Women's Aboriginal Program at Elizabeth Fry Society of Edmonton; and Colleen Novotny, Coordinator, Internal Operations, Boyle McCauley Health Centre.

I thank the project funder, Adult Learning, Literacy and Essential Skills Program, Human Resources and Social Development Canada, for its support. ●

Thank you!

Judy Murphy
Project Manager and Author
Easy-to-Read Health Series

(Welcome

We all live in relationships of one kind or another. We might share our homes with family members or friends. Some of us work with many different people. Some of us have gone back to school to learn with others. No matter what kind of relationships we have, they are an important part of our lives. In fact, we can't live without them. Most basic of all is our relationship with ourselves.

This book is about relationships. It talks about relationships with people who are close to you—a partner or spouse, someone you are dating, your family members, or friends. It helps you think about whether your relationships are healthy. It helps you decide whether you want to keep or end a relationship. It

♣ **food for thought**
It takes both rain and sunshine to make a rainbow.

— Anonymous

A healthy relationship

- feels like soft mist
  off a waterfall

- feels like being at the
  top of a Ferris wheel

- feels like floating
  on a cloud

- sounds like the
  ice cream buggy

- smells like fresh flowers
  in the rain

- tastes like a Tim Horton
  coffee in the morning

An unhealthy relationship

- looks like a black thick
  thundercloud

- looks like a pond
  in the muskeg

- feels like an icy thick fog

- smells like old fungus

- tastes like dried toast

— Participants in a writing and
  reading class at Learning
  Connections, The Learning
  Centre Literacy Association

suggests some ways to strengthen your relationships and enjoy them more—both relationships with others and yourself. This book will help you to understand how to:

- tell the difference between healthy and unhealthy relationships.
- respond to and resolve conflict.
- communicate with others.
- build healthy relationships.

(1 Understanding Relationships

What does it mean to be in a relationship? What does it feel like? What does it look like? When does it feel good? When does it feel painful?

What does a healthy relationship look like?

There are three parts to a relationship: I, YOU, and WE. In a healthy relationship, these three parts are balanced.

I

I know what I need.
I know what I want.
I can fulfill my goals.

WE

We respect each other's needs and wants.

We support each other without losing our individual identity.

YOU

I care about what you need.
I care about what you want.

I can help you solve problems without giving up my needs and wants.

In healthy relationships, people trust, respect, and care for each other. Each person in the relationship is equal. One person does not have more control or power than the other.

In a healthy relationship, we can be authentic. This means we can say what we believe, think, and feel. We do not need to act differently or pretend to feel different to please the other person. If we feel relaxed enough to be authentic, we tend to grow closer to the other person.

A healthy relationship is balanced. This means being able to shift from "I" to "You" to "We." For example, you might focus on your "I" if you go back to school or start a new job. You might shift your focus to "You" if a family member or friend is sick and needs your care. You might be in your "We" space as you plan a birthday with your partner.

Balance also means both people in a relationship come together as two individuals with their own hopes and dreams. They can be together and separate at the same time.

Healthy and unhealthy relationships

People often talk about relationships as being healthy or unhealthy. This sounds as if there might be a right way or a wrong way to be in a relationship. Or it sounds as if a relationship is either good or bad. In reality, no relationship is perfect. Most relationships slide back and forth between being healthy and unhealthy.

Relationships

Healthy   Unhealthy

Trusting
Respectful
Caring

Painful
Unsafe

What are the signs of a healthy relationship?

The following signs provide us with a tool for thinking about our relationships.

A relationship is healthy when both people—	Examples
trust and support each other	They help each other in hard times. They support each other's goals. They feel safe with each other.
show respect and kindness	They value each other's ideas and opinions. They respect each other's feelings, friends, and activities.
are honest and open with each other	They can admit mistakes to each other. They feel comfortable talking about their feelings.
share responsibilities	They make important decisions together. They share the workload.
use good communication skills	They listen to each other. They fight fairly.
enjoy time together and apart	They set aside time to be together. They have their own friends and interests. They have separate identities.

A healthy relationship makes us feel safe, happy, confident, and trusted. Being in a healthy relationship leads to a healthier life.

How healthy is your relationship?

Think about an important relationship in your life.
Answer the questions by checking *yes* or *no*.

Does the other person—	YES	NO
feel happy that you have other friends?		
feel happy about good things that happen to you?		
respect your opinions and decisions?		
listen to you?		
support your hopes and dreams?		
have their own friends and interests?		
take responsibility for their decisions and actions?		
share the daily chores with you?		
make you feel safe?		
share the same beliefs and values?		

If you answered most of these questions with a yes, you are
probably in a healthy relationship. If you answered most of these
questions with a no, you may be in an unhealthy relationship.

A healthy relationship means respecting the other person. It means being honest and supportive of the other person. But first, you need to respect, be honest with, and be supportive of yourself.

How healthy is your relationship with yourself?

Your self-esteem affects your life in many ways. If you have high self-esteem, you feel confident and good about yourself. When you like yourself, it is easier to have healthy relationships with others.

Self-esteem Scale[1]

Let's look at your feelings about yourself.

Read each statement. If you strongly agree with the statement, circle SA. If you agree, circle A. If you disagree, circle D. If you strongly disagree, circle SD.

	Strongly Agree	Agree	Disagree	Strongly Disagree
1. I feel that I am a person of worth, at least the equal of others.	SA	A	D	SD
2. I feel that I have a number of good qualities.	SA	A	D	SD
3. All in all, I seem to feel that I am a failure.	SA	A	D	SD
4. I am able to do things as well as most other people.	SA	A	D	SD
5. I feel I do not have much to be proud of.	SA	A	D	SD
6. I take a positive attitude toward myself.	SA	A	D	SD
7. On the whole, I am satisfied with myself.	SA	A	D	SD
8. I wish I could have more respect for myself.	SA	A	D	SD
9. I certainly feel useless at times.	SA	A	D	SD
10. At times I think I am no good at all.	SA	A	D	SD

How you feel about yourself can change depending on your relationship with others. Being in a healthy relationship can help you build your self-esteem. When you stay in an unhealthy relationship, you might find it harder to have a high level of self-esteem.

You can build your self-esteem by

> accepting every part of yourself
> being true to yourself
> having self-respect
> taking responsibility for your actions
> taking time for yourself.

By building high self-esteem we learn to care for ourselves. If we have high self-esteem, we find it easier to have healthy relationships with others.

Summary

A healthy relationship is based on respect and kindness.

In a healthy relationship, people

- trust and support each other
- are honest and open
- share responsibilities
- use good communication skills
- have fun together
- feel like they can be themselves
- share similar values and beliefs
- have different interests and opinions
- enjoy time together and apart
- support each other's hopes and dreams •

2 Knowing Yourself

We all need to know who we are. We all need to know how we got to where we are today. And we all need to know how to change for the better.

It is impossible to change someone else. But we can control and change ourselves.

As the Serenity Prayer says,

> Give me the serenity to accept the things I cannot change,
> the courage to change the things I can,
> and the wisdom to know the difference.

❖ **food for thought**

You must be the change
you wish to see in the world.

—Mahatma Gandhi

Understanding past relationships

How were you treated as a child? Your childhood experiences can shape how you treat others. Your childhood will have an impact on your relationships. Your early experiences shape and colour your new experiences.

CAUTION

The following activity can raise strong, even painful, emotions if your childhood was unhappy or abusive. Before you begin, think about what helps you to feel safe. Where do you want to be while you do the activities? Do you want to do the activities alone or with a friend? If you choose to do these activities, notice how you are feeling. Stop whenever you don't feel safe or if you feel too uncomfortable.

Important Relationships in Your Youth[2]

STEP 1

Find a quiet place. Sit in a comfortable chair. You can close your eyes or keep them open. If you prefer to keep your eyes open, look gently down towards your heart. Take a full, deep breath. When you breathe out, say "Relax." Imagine you are blowing away all your tension and stress. When you breathe in, say "Peace." Imagine you are breathing in calmness. Keep doing this for a few minutes. Then go back to your normal breath. Do you notice a difference from when you started the activity?

STEP 2

Continue to sit with your eyes closed or open. Think about three people who were important to you as you were growing up. If you feel safe, imagine spending a few moments with each person. If you don't want them to reach you, imagine there is a large piece of glass that separates you from them. Imagine you have a chance to talk with each of them. This is your chance to talk as they cannot respond.

Tell each of them,

> what you liked about them
> what you didn't like about them
> how your relationship with them made you feel
> why you are thankful for knowing them
> how they let you down

STEP 3

Look at the circle.
In Part A, list the things you liked about them.
In Part B, list the things that you didn't like about them.

A

B

STEP 4

Look at what you wrote in Part A of the circle.
Which three words have the most meaning for you?
Circle them.

Look at what you wrote in Part B of the circle.
Which three words have the most meaning for you?
Circle them.

STEP 5

Complete these two sentences with your thoughts:

(a) As a child, what I wanted most in my relationships was

_____ .

(b) As a child, I felt _____ when my needs
were not met.

♣ **food for thought**

The best relationship is the one
in which your love for each other
exceeds your need for each other.

—Anonymous

Read the questions in Column A.
Follow the directions in Column B to answer them.

Column A	Column B
What qualities do you want in a partner or friend?	Copy the 3 words you circled in Part A of the circle. _____ _____ _____
What qualities in a partner or friend make you feel bad?	Copy the 3 words you circled in Part B of the circle. _____ _____ _____
What do you need most from your partner or friend?	Copy your answer to 5a. _____
How do you feel when your partner or friend does not give you what you need?	Copy your answer to 5b. _____

STEP 7

Think about this activity.
    What did you learn?
    What surprises you?
    How do you feel about your answers?

Think about your current relationships.
In what ways are they similar to your childhood relationships?

My identity[3]

How would you respond to the question, "Who am I?" Is your identity defined by your relationship with others? For example, do you identify yourself as a wife or husband, mother or father, sister or brother or friend? Sometimes, our relationships with others become more important than our relationship with ourselves. When this happens, we lose sight of who we are.

Our identity is complex. It consists of three parts: social identity, chosen identity, and core identity. Each part of our identity is described on the next page.

♣ **food for thought**

Self-knowledge has no end—you don't come to an achievement, you don't come to a conclusion. It is an endless river.

—Krishnamurti

Social Identity

Our social identity is who "we" are in relation to "others." Our social identity includes our race, gender, and class. Our social identity affects how we think and act in relationships.

Chosen Identity

♣ **food for thought**

It's not the events of our lives that shape us, but our beliefs as to what those events mean.

—Anthony Robbins

Our chosen identity consists of choices that we make in our life. Our chosen identity includes our roles, skills, hobbies, work, religion, and lifestyle choices. Our chosen identity helps us to make connections with other people.

Core Identity

Our core identity is what makes us unique—it is our true self. Our core identity includes values, beliefs, and behaviour. Our core identity is how we perceive ourselves. Core values are the glue that holds relationships together.

In this next activity, you can look at the different parts of your identity. You will see that you are much more than a wife/husband, mother/father, sister/brother or friend.

Mapping Your Identity

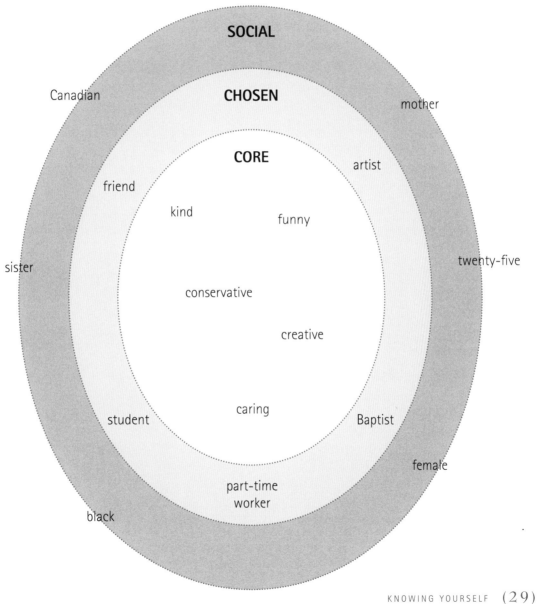

SOCIAL

CHOSEN

Canadian

mother

CORE

artist

friend

kind

funny

sister

twenty-five

conservative

creative

caring

student

Baptist

part-time
worker

female

black

STEP 1

Look at the completed map that contains examples. Draw your own map. In the outer ring, write words that describe your **social identity.**

STEP 2

In the next ring, list all the aspects of your **chosen identity.**

STEP 3

In the centre of the map, write the words that describe your personality or **core identity.** Are you kind, funny, impatient, etc.?

STEP 4

After you complete your map, circle the items that are important to you.

Look at the circled items. Are they part of your social, chosen, or core identity? What aspects of your identity help you to make strong relationships with other people? How would you answer the question, "Who am I?"

♣ **food for thought**

We are the hero of our own story.

—Mary McCarthy

Exploring My Identity

Look at the chart.
Complete the sentences with your ideas.

What brings me joy?	When I'm alone, I enjoy _____ . When I'm with friends, I enjoy _____ . When I'm with family, I enjoy _____ . My hobbies are _____ . My favourite thing to do is _____ . I am interested in _____ .
What are my strengths?	What I like most about myself is _____ . I'm good at _____ . A good thing I have done is _____ . I am at my best when _____ .
What brings me sorrow?	I feel sad when _____ . When I feel sad, I _____ so I feel better.
How do I relate to others?	I show people I care about them by _____ . I help people to understand me by _____ . The people I care about most are _____ . I feel best with a person when _____ . I feel good when people say I _____ .

Were you able to complete the sentences? Do you think you know yourself? How often do you think about who you are?

Review your answers. Complete each of the following sentences with one main idea that describes who you are or what you want.

I am _____.

I want _____.

People with a strong self-identity know who they are and what they want.

You might not be aware of your needs and wants. You might get caught up in doing the best you can with all the things you have to do in a day. Sometimes, your busy life can prevent you from listening to yourself and paying attention to your thoughts and feelings. You can easily lose touch with your true self. When you have a chance to become still and quiet, you have a better chance of clearly seeing who you really are. You can reflect on what you need and want, what matters to you, and what you dream about. •

Loss of the sacred and the
honour of being who I am—
a spirit, a child, a woman.
The innocence of childhood, a rocky ride
The urgency to grow up are forced upon me
No ceremonies welcoming me into womanhood—
Only shame washed over me.

Finding the healing in water, cleansing my soul
Reflection of true spirit and sacredness
Reflections of dreams and
Pieces of puzzles which slip easily into place
Re-healing the ripples as God naturally
intended them to be—sacred.

Like the houses on an island with
colours as beautiful as the rainbow
A promise of coming home.
A treasure unfolds.
A coming home on calm waters in a
vessel strong and safe and sacred.

—Maggie M.

❦ **food for thought**

Friendship with oneself is
all-important, because without
it one cannot be friends with
anyone else in the world.

—Eleanor Roosevelt

(3 Responding to Conflict

Every person is unique. Each of us has our own set of values, attitudes, needs, and beliefs. Sometimes, we accept another person's differences. At other times, we disagree with what another person says or does. These disagreements are called conflicts.

Most people experience conflict in relationships. Sometimes, conflict can be a positive experience. Conflict can lead to new ways of thinking. Conflict can be a chance to grow or learn. At other times, conflict can be a negative experience. Such conflict can lead to verbal abuse and even violent behaviour.

♣ food for thought

Arguing better than someone else does not make you right, it just makes you better at arguing.

—Unknown

(35)

What causes conflict?

There are four common causes of conflict: responsibilities, values, resources, and change.

Common causes of conflict	Example	Add a personal example
Responsibilities	Family members argue about whose turn it is to do the dishes.	
Values/Beliefs	Parents argue about how to discipline children.	
Resources (e.g., time, money)	Partners disagree about how to spend their money.	
Change	Employees get upset if their job description changes.	

Think about the conflicts with the important people in your life. What were the conflicts really about? Were they about responsibility? Were they about different values? Were they about how to use limited resources such as time or money? Or were they about changes in daily routines or life?

What is your conflict style?

There are many ways to respond to conflict. Some people always respond to conflict in the same way. For example, one might always try to be a peacemaker. Another might always try to "win" the fight by yelling or using violence. Other people respond to conflict in different ways. Their response to conflict depends on the situation and how comfortable they are with the other person.

Here is a checklist to see what conflict style you use the most.[4] Read each statement. Check the statement that describes your behaviour.

♣ **food for thought**

I've learned that people will forget what you said, people will forget what you did, but people will never forget how you made them feel.

—Maya Angelou

Box #	When I am in a conflict, I	Always	Usually	Some-times	Never
1.	will give up what I want, including my relationship, in order to avoid conflict.	—	—	—	—
	hope the problems will go away.	—	—	—	—
	won't say what I think, even if I know what is right.	—	—	—	—
	walk away.	—	—	—	—
2.	look at what each side could give up.	—	—	—	—
	look for ways to keep both the relationship and what I want.	—	—	—	—
	will give up some things in exchange for other things.	—	—	—	—
	try to find a middle ground.	—	—	—	—
			continued next page		

Box #	When I am in a conflict, I	Always	Usually	Some-times	Never
3.	put the other person's feelings before mine. am willing to go along with others. will not argue if it makes others feel bad. will give up what I want to keep the peace.	— — — —	— — — —	— — — —	— — — —
4.	try to understand why people want things. want to share my feelings and ideas, and I want to hear the ideas and feelings of others. want to make sure that everyone gets what they need. want to hear all sides before working out a solution.	— — — —	— — — —	— — — —	— — — —
5.	try to win because I know that I am right. keep pushing until I make my point. stick to what I want, no matter how the other person feels. am ready to use force if needed.	— — — —	— — — —	— — — —	— — — —

What is your *main* conflict style?

_____

>> Read more about these conflict styles on the following five pages.

Box #	Total "always" and "usually" answers for each box.	Conflict Style
1		Avoider
2		Deal-maker
3		Care-taker
4		Problem-solver
5		Steam-roller

The Avoider

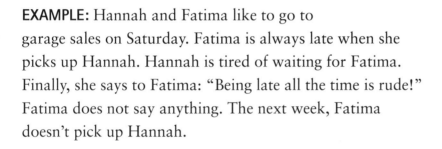

GOAL: To avoid conflict and keep the peace.

RESPONSE TO CONFLICT: Avoiders withdraw from conflict by walking away or being silent.

COMMON LANGUAGE: "Can we talk about this some other time?"

EXAMPLE: Hannah and Fatima like to go to garage sales on Saturday. Fatima is always late when she picks up Hannah. Hannah is tired of waiting for Fatima. Finally, she says to Fatima: "Being late all the time is rude!" Fatima does not say anything. The next week, Fatima doesn't pick up Hannah.

Who is the Avoider in this example?

_____

RESOLVING CONFLICT WITH AVOIDERS:

- Give avoiders time and space to think about the issue.
- Set a time to meet with them and talk about the issue.

The Deal-maker

GOAL: To find a solution to the conflict by meeting the needs of both people.

RESPONSE TO CONFLICT: Deal-makers listen to the other person before expressing their own needs.

COMMON LANGUAGE: "I'll do …, if you do …."

EXAMPLE: Carlos and Maria have lived together for six years. Carlos works full-time and Maria stays at home with their baby. Maria thinks that Carlos is not doing enough around the house. Maria is always cleaning up after Carlos. Maria tells Carlos that she does not want to clean up his mess. Maria says she will do the household chores if he agrees to pick up after himself. Carlos agrees to pick up after himself. Maria agrees to keep doing the majority of household chores.

Who is the Deal-maker in this example?

_____

RESOLVING CONFLICT WITH DEAL-MAKERS:

- Be prepared to give and take with deal-makers.
- Try to find a practical solution.
- Think and speak in terms of "being fair" and "reasonable."

The Care-taker

GOAL: To please the other person, even if it means neglecting personal needs.

RESPONSE TO CONFLICT: Care-takers usually accept the other person's point of view because they worry conflict might damage their relationship.

COMMON LANGUAGE: "Whatever you want is fine with me."

EXAMPLE: Corizan and Rodel are getting married. Rodel's mother wants them to have a big wedding. Corizan would prefer to have a small wedding in their backyard. Corizan wants to keep peace in the family. She doesn't want her future mother-in-law to get angry at her. Corizan agrees to have a big wedding.

Who is the Care-taker in this example?

_____

RESOLVING CONFLICT WITH CARE-TAKERS:

- Talk about how you value your relationship with them.
- Connect at a human level (ask how they are doing, ask about a family member) before you talk about the conflict.
- Encourage care-takers to express their needs openly.

The Steam-roller

GOAL: To win the conflict and gain power by meeting their own needs at the expense of the other person.

RESPONSE TO CONFLICT: Steam-rollers argue, lose their tempers, raise their voices, use violence, or the threat of violence.

COMMON LANGUAGE: "We're doing it my way."

EXAMPLE: Lara owns a cleaning company. The company uses toxic cleaning products. Terry, an employee, meets with Lara. Terry suggests that the company use products that do not harm the environment. Lara gets angry at the suggestion. She tells Terry to mind his own business. Lara tells Terry to find another job if he's unhappy.

Who is the Steam-roller in this example?

_____

RESOLVING CONFLICT WITH STEAM-ROLLERS:

- If the steam-roller has a history of abuse, avoid conflict, or look for a path to safety or shelter.
- If the steam-roller is emotionally healthy, let them know you want to resolve the conflict. Set a time to talk about the issue.

The Problem-solver

GOAL: To find a win/win solution that pleases both people.

RESPONSE TO CONFLICT: Problem-solvers ask questions and listen to the other person's wants, needs, and concerns.

COMMON LANGUAGE: "I want to solve this in a way that makes both of us happy."

EXAMPLE: Stacey and Anna live near a park. There are many homeless people who live in the park. They live in tents. Stacey thinks the homeless people should find another place to live. Anna does not agree with Stacey. Anna organizes a community meeting to see how everybody feels about the homeless people.

Who is the Problem-solver in this example?

_____

RESOLVING CONFLICT WITH PROBLEM-SOLVERS

- Be direct about what you need and want.
- Tell problem-solvers you want to hear about their concerns.

Read the example. Then, think of two conflicts you have experienced.

Fill in the chart based on these experiences.

	Example	Conflict #1	Conflict #2
Who was the conflict with?	Partner		
What was the conflict about?	He wasn't helping enough with the kids.		
What was the cause of the conflict? (See page 36)	Resources (time)		
How did you deal with the conflict?	I asked him how he felt about his time with the kids.		
What was your conflict style? (See pages 39 to 43)	Problem-solver		
What was the result?	He'll watch a movie with them once in a while but that's it.		

Review your answers for each conflict.

What was the conflict style of the other person?

Are you happy with the result? If no, what can be changed so you get a more positive result next time?

Summary

The Problem-solver and the Deal-maker styles are the best ways to work through conflict. The Problem-solver style tries to fulfill the needs and wants of both people. The Deal-maker style works well when both people need a quick solution and both sides are willing to give up something.

The other three styles can have a negative impact on people. If Avoiders continue to withdraw from conflict, they might feel powerless or angry. They may express their anger towards someone at another time. Because Care-takers usually ignore their own feelings and values, they might begin to hold a grudge against the other person.

♣ food for thought

The quality of our lives depends not on whether or not we have conflicts, but on how we respond to them.

—Tom Crum

Steam-rollers are not effective at resolving conflict. Their style often results in fights. You need to set boundaries if you have a relationship with a Steam-roller.

Setting boundaries

♣ food for thought

Your personal boundaries protect the inner core of your identity and your right to choices.

—Gerard Manley Hopkins

Sometimes, conflicts cause people to fight. People fight in different ways. Some people raise their voices. Others show their anger through verbal or physical abuse. To deepen close relationships, we need to set boundaries when we fight.

We need to find out

(1) how the other person feels about fighting
(2) what kind of fighting feels okay for the other person
(3) what the other person needs at the end of a fight

Read the examples. Complete these three sentences with your own ideas.

	Complete the sentences.	Examples
When we fight, I feel it is okay to—		be honest, even if it might hurt a little.
When we fight, I feel it is not okay to—		call each other names.
When we finish fighting, I need—		a few minutes by myself.

Dealing with conflict

There are healthy and unhealthy ways to respond to conflict. On the next page, unhealthy responses are listed in the left-hand column. List a healthy response in the right-hand column.

Unhealthy Responses to Conflict	Healthy Response
say things like "You always—" or "You never—"	Use "I" statements. • I feel upset about ...
bring up all past problems and hurts at one time	
criticize the other person just because the other person criticizes you	
believe you are blameless	
believe that only the other person needs to change	
walk away or give the silent treatment	
say the issue is not important	
change the subject	
pretend to agree and then try to make things go your way later	
say everything is fine but act cold or rude to the other person	
pretend to be sad so the other person feels sorry for you	
ignore the conflict	

Add other responses to the lists.

Summary

It is important to work through conflict in ways that do not hurt either person. This is not the same as being "nice" all the time and giving up your beliefs. People are strong when they have a good sense of who they are and what is important to them. They can be strong on the inside and gentle on the outside. In a healthy relationship, conflict can be balanced by humour, love, caring, and respect. ●

❖ food for thought

...the power of a touch, a smile, a kind word, a listening ear, an honest compliment, or the smallest act of caring, all of which have the potential to turn a life around.

—Leo Buscaglia

4 Resolving Conflicts

Good communication skills are the key to resolving conflicts. Active listening can help bring clarity and understanding to disagreements. An active listener allows the other person to communicate their ideas and opinions. Trying to understand the other person's point of view helps to build and establish trust. The other side of listening is talking. Constructive talking can deepen the understanding and connection with the other person in the relationship.

Are you an active listener?

The quiz on the next page will help you learn about your listening skills. Read each statement and rate your listening skills. Do you want a second opinion? If so, ask another person to rate your listening skills.

Active Listening Quiz [5]

Listening Skills	Never	Sometimes	Often	Usually	Always
I clear my mind of personal worries and concerns before entering the conversation.					
I continue to pay attention even when the other person talks a lot.					
I focus on the other's person's conversation even when I do not think it is relevant.					
I wait for the other person to finish before thinking about my response.					
I am comfortable with silence and allow time for the other person to think.					
If I don't understand, I ask the other person to repeat or clarify what they said.					
I don't finish the other person's sentences for them.					
I don't interrupt, even if I think I know what the other person is saying. I let them finish.					
I don't multi-task. All of my attention is on the other person.					
I can continue to listen, even if the other person presents information that I disagree with.					

Are most of your answers "usually" or "always"? If so, you are probably a pretty good listener.

Active listening is listening with a purpose. An active listener hears the speaker's message, understands the meaning of the message, and confirms the meaning by offering feedback. When people are active listeners, they

- do not judge what the other person is saying
- spend more time listening than talking
- focus on what is being said, not their response
- let the other person finish speaking before responding
- use positive non-verbal cues (e.g., maintain eye contact)
- encourage the other person to talk openly by saying, "I see" or "Can you tell me more—"
- ask questions to make sure they understand
- restate the other person's message in their own words
- restate the other person's basic feelings
- summarize the other person's important ideas

Listen + Clarify and Understand + Confirm Meaning = **ACTIVE LISTENING**

How to listen when the truth hurts

How do you respond to criticism?

Read each point in the chart.[6] Tick the points that describe you.

	When I feel that the other person is criticizing me, I
	1. get anxious and cannot think straight.
	2. keep quiet but will get back at the other person later.
	3. believe it is mostly my fault.
	4. listen but say nothing.
	5. change the subject.
	6. become very sad or cry.
	7. get mad and tell the other person they are wrong.
	8. shut down and stop listening.
	9. start to criticize the other person.
	10. pay attention to what the other person is saying so I can learn more about what they feel or what worries them.
	11. ask for a time-out if I am upset. I tell the other person that I need time to get in touch with my own feelings before I give them my full attention.
	12. feel good about the fact that the other person is honest.

Do you have tick marks beside points 10 to 12?
If yes, you react in a positive way when you feel that the other person is criticizing you.

Do you have tick marks beside points 1 to 9?
If yes, here are three ways you can prepare yourself to hear criticism in a positive way.

❖ food for thought

Smile: if you can't lift the corners, let the middle sag.

—Unknown

1. **Tell each other three things that you like about each other or value in the relationship.** Starting the discussion in a positive way helps set the stage. You will be more open to what the other person says.

2. **Remember that the other person is not your enemy.** The other person wants to resolve a conflict, not hurt you.

3. **Put yourself in the other person's shoes.** Imagine how they see the situation. Imagine how they feel.

People find it hard to listen when they are being criticized. Many people get defensive. They think the other person is wrong. Others listen to criticism and look for what's true.

The gift of listening

Have you ever had another person really listen to you?
How did you feel?

One of the most special gifts we can give another
person is to listen carefully to what they have to say.
The next time you have a conversation with another
person, notice if you pay close attention to what they
are saying. For example, do you look at them while they
are talking? Do you just pretend to listen while you are
thinking of something else? Or do you look around the
room, glance at your watch, or reach into your pocket
for something?

Listening is one of the hardest things to do well. When
we listen actively to another person, we learn more about
them. We begin to understand what they feel, need and
want. Listening tells the other person that we think they
are important. Listening tells them we care. Listening
shows them we are interested in what they have to say.

Practice and patience will help you become a better
listener.

Try this activity with someone you feel comfortable with. One person is the listener; the other is the speaker. The speaker chooses a simple topic—their day at work or school, their children, or what they do in their free time—and talks for three minutes. The listener does nothing except listen actively to what the speaker is saying. At the end of the three minutes, switch roles.

Share what it felt like to be listened to by an active listener. Did it feel special? Did it feel good to have non-stop attention? Share what it felt like to be an active listener. Was it hard to do at times? Why?

Constructive talking

Constructive talking creates a two-way door between you and another person. Here are three constructive ways of talking that are easy to learn and practice.

1. Begin your sentences with "I."

- *I feel angry about—*
- *I feel sad when—*
- *I was embarrassed when—*

Using "I" helps you
     feel strong.

❖ food for thought

When love listens, it listens with an ear and a heart to the unspoken.

—Daphne Rose Kingma

Using "I" helps the other person
    feel more comfortable.
    feel less under attack.

Read the pairs of sentences.
Which sentence sounds softer?

1 (a) You're always late. You make me so mad.

   (b) I feel mad when you're late. I feel ignored.

2 (a) I feel sad when you don't say hello to my kids.

   (b) You never say hello to my kids. Don't you
      like them?

3 (a) You embarrass me when you swear in front
      of my mother.

   (b) I feel embarrassed when you swear in front
      of my mother. Can you try to stop, please?

> Use "I."
> State your feeling.
> Give a reason for your feeling.
> Suggest what you would like the person to do.

2. Be honest and open.

Express your feelings and thoughts as clearly as possible. Admit where you need to change.

3. Keep talking with each other.

A healthy relationship depends on two people being able to talk together. When you stop talking, conflict can become more serious.

> Some conflict is never solved.
> In this case, agree to disagree.
> But always respect your differences.

✤ **food for thought**
We are each of us angels with only one wing, and we can only fly by embracing one another.

—Luciano de Crescenzo

Summary

Conflict resolution depends on both people in the relationship having good communication skills. Active listening shows you respect the other person, even if they have something negative to say. Constructive talking shows that you care about how the other person feels. Constructive talking also shows the other person that you feel comfortable enough in the relationship to express your wants and needs openly and honestly. ●

5 Ending a Relationship

Many people end a relationship because they have grown apart. Some people *want* to end a relationship because it is not working out. Other people *must* end a relationship because they are being abused. Do you ever think about ending an important relationship? It's a difficult decision to make. Sometimes, making the decision is harder than ending the relationship. How do you make and carry out such a difficult decision?

How do you end a relationship?

It is hard and painful to end a relationship, even if it is the right decision. The suggestions that follow can help lessen the pain of ending a relationship.

1. Choose the right time and place.

Before you break the bad news, give the person a warning sign. You can say, "We need to talk about something important." Then, choose a time and place that works for both of you. Avoid breaking up on a special day, like a birthday or holiday. Also, avoid breaking up on a hard day, such as before an exam.

2. Be prepared.

Prepare yourself for the other person's emotions. The other person might cry, yell, or remain silent. Allow the person time to share their feelings. Listen and remain calm.

3. Establish boundaries for the future.

Do you want to end the relationship? Or do you want to change the nature of the relationship? Be clear about whether you want to see the person in the future. If you want to remain friends, you should allow each other some time and space to grieve.

4. Take responsibility.

It is easy to blame the other person for the problems and upsets in the relationship. You need to take responsibility for your role in the relationship. This is a chance to be honest with yourself. Being honest takes courage.

Ending a relationship is hard, even if you are the one who wants to end it. Give yourself time to feel hurt, sad, or angry. If you do not grieve, the negative feelings will stay with you and affect your other relationships. Understand that the other person needs time to grieve as well.

♣ food for thought

Failure is only the opportunity to begin again, this time more wisely.

—Unknown

Ending a relationship respectfully and thoughtfully
is the first step in being able
to move forward in your life.

Abusive relationships

How do you end an abusive relationship?

Abuse can happen between partners, spouses, and family members. Even friends can be abusive with each other. Abuse can happen in the workplace or with a neighbour. Abuse is a pattern of behaviour used to establish power and control over another person. Three common types of abuse are physical, mental, and sexual. The abuse usually gets worse over a period of time. The power and control wheel[7] describes men's abusive behaviour toward women.

Men suffer abuse and violence from women, as well. However, women are five to eight times more likely to be abused by men. This chapter refers to abusers as "he."

Power and Control Wheel

VIOLENCE *physical* *sexual*

Coercion & Threats
- making and/or carrying out threats to hurt her
- making threats to leave her, commit suicide
- making her drop charges against him
- making her do illegal things

Intimidation
- making her afraid
- destroying her property
- abusing pets
- displaying weapons

Male Privilege
- treating her like a servant
- making all the big decisions
- being the one to define men's and women's roles

Emotional Abuse
- making her feel bad about herself
- calling her names
- making her think she's crazy
- making her feel guilty

POWER AND CONTROL

Economic Abuse
- preventing her from getting or keeping a job
- making her ask for money
- giving her an allowance
- taking her money

Isolation
- controlling what she does, who she sees and talks to, what she reads
- limiting her outside involvement

Using Children
- making her feel guilty about the children
- using the children to relay messages
- threatening to take the children away

Minimizing, Denying, & Blaming
- not taking her concerns about abuse seriously
- saying the abuse didn't happen
- shifting responsibility for abusive behaviour

VIOLENCE *physical* *sexual*

Make a safety plan

If you decide to end an abusive relationship, you need to make a **safety plan**. This plan will help you protect yourself and your children, and others for whom you are responsible.

Ask yourself the following questions:

- Who can help me? How can they help me?
- Where can I stay? Where can I keep my children safe?
- What do I need to take with me?
- How much money will I need?
- How do I ensure my safety once I leave?

Plan to leave the abuser when he is not at home. If you stay in the same community,

- Avoid staying alone
- Change your routines
- Tell your employer about your situation
- Screen your phone calls

- Inform your children's schools and let teachers know who will be picking up your children
- Avoid places that you went to when you were together (e.g., banks, stores)

Most communities have services such as

- help lines
- women's shelters
- counselling services
- support services

These services will help you make and carry out your **safety plan**.

❖ food for thought

Hope is the thing with feathers that perches in the soul.

—Emily Dickinson

Abuse can be physical, sexual, or emotional.

Abusive relationships don't happen between only spouses and partners. Abuse can be a part of a relationship with a child, friend, co-worker, neighbour, or boss.

Why do people stay in abusive relationships?

When safety becomes an issue, the relationship must end. Yet, some abused people find it hard to end the relationship.

Do you know someone who is being abused? Do you wonder why the person stays in the relationship? Some women stay because they feel responsible for making the relationship work. For others, the fear of leaving is greater than the fear of staying.

Many women stay in abusive relationships because they fear poverty. Many abused women have at least one child. They want custody of their children. These mothers do not know how they will support their families.

Some women fear their abusers will become more violent if they leave. An abused woman might feel like she has nowhere to turn for help. She might not be aware of shelters that provide safety. Or, she might not be aware of community services, such as help lines.

Eight years it lasted. In the beginning, it was like a honeymoon. I was everything. I was his world. We laughed and we smiled. We talked and he held me when I cried. He held me for no reason. It was like a rainbow that shone through the mist of a waterfall.

In time, about three years into our relationship, it all started to crumble and release itself into a dark empty hole to be held back and kept hidden like a mushroom under a log. I lost family and friends who knew nothing. I help myself up and kept going.

>>>

Some women fear the unknown. A woman may think, "What if I fall into another relationship where the abuse is even worse?" By remaining in her current abusive relationship, she thinks she knows what to expect.

Finally, many women feel isolated from their friends and family. This is because abusers control a woman's relationships with others. Many abusers decide who a woman can see and talk to. An abused woman feels alone in the world. She might stay in a bad relationship because she believes that having a bad partner is better than being alone.

> As we neared the end of the seventh year, I knew I had to leave all the violence, pain and hurt. It was hard, but to end a fight was a win and a loss—to regain who I was and who I was to be, ending good but also ending bad for my family and myself.
>
> —Debbie Lathlin

How can you come to terms with the break-up?

Going through a break-up is an emotional time. It is a time to be honest with yourself. It is a time to reflect and learn. Below are some suggestions to help you come to terms with the breakup.

1. Express your feelings

It is important to express your feelings while going through a breakup.

> Keep a journal.
> Talk to a friend or family member you trust.
> See a counsellor.

♣ **food for thought**

Life is not the way it's supposed to be. It's the way it is. The way you cope with it is what makes the difference.

—Virginia Satir

2. Find the good

Think of all the things you learned from your relationship. Think of all the things you learned by having the courage to leave. Make a list. Keep adding to the list as you think of more things.

What I learned from the relationship	What I learned from leaving the relationship
I can handle money well. I am loyal. I need to respect my feelings more.	I am a very good mother. I can take care of myself. I'm strong enough to make hard decisions.

3. Forgive yourself

Do you feel that

   you stayed in the relationship too long?
   your children suffered in the relationship?
   you could have done things differently?
   you hurt people during the relationship?

Admit your wrongs and your regrets. Forgive yourself.
You did the best you could at a difficult time. •

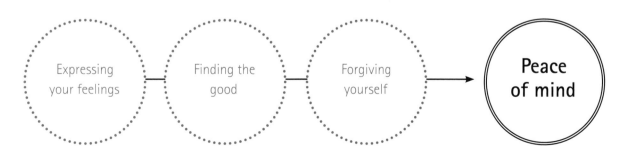

Expressing your feelings → Finding the good → Forgiving yourself → **Peace of mind**

(6 Building Healthy Relationships

In a healthy relationship, people use good communication skills to share ideas and feelings. People also establish personal boundaries that define what they will and will not accept in the behaviour of others.

A healthy relationship feels alive. It is full of fun, excitement, and energy. People find the positive in each other. People find ways to spend time together. This chapter focuses on building healthy relationships with the important people in your life.

Personal boundaries

Personal boundaries are the limits we set in relationships. These limits define what we will and will not accept in other people's behaviour. These boundaries are our invisible lines of protection. We need to be able to tell other people when they are acting in ways that are not acceptable to us.

Boundaries separate our identities from the identities of others. Boundaries make it possible for us to separate our own thoughts and feelings from those of others. Boundaries make it possible for us to take responsibility for what we think, feel, and do.

Boundaries come from having a good sense of our own self-worth. When we lack a sense of our own identity, we tend to draw our identity from the other person. We can't imagine who we would be without our relationship with the other person. Boundaries are the lines that say where the "I" begins and ends in a relationship.

Knowing Your Personal Boundaries

Check off the boxes that are true for you in columns A
and B.

	Column A	Column B	
✓	**Do you—**	**Do you—**	✓
	feel you are living a life that someone else wants and not what you dream about for yourself?	feel you are living the life that is right for you?	
	change the things you want to do to match the other person's mood or wishes?	respect the other person's wishes and feelings while staying true to what feels right to you?	
	have a hard time saying "no" when the other person asks you to do something you really do not want to do?	say "no" with confidence when you feel you need to?	
	do more and more for the other person and less and less for yourself?	know when to do more for the other person and when to do more for yourself?	
	often feel hurt and helpless but not angry?	let yourself feel anger and see what can be done to change things?	
	often feel anxious and afraid?	feel safe and cared for?	

continued next page

	Column A	Column B	
✓	**Do you—**	**Do you—**	**✓**
	allow the other person to abuse a family member, child, or friend?	ensure the other person knows what is unacceptable behaviour toward other people in your life?	
	make excuses for the other person for things they say or do that do not feel right to you?	refuse to accept behaviour that feels wrong?	
	depend on the other person to make you happy?	create fun and excitement for you and the other person?	
	feel you have to tell everything to the other person?	decide what to keep to yourself and what to share with the other person?	
	question/doubt what you want or need?	know what you want and need?	
	often wait for the other person to guess what you need?	ask for what you want and need?	

If you checked off more boxes in column A, you probably have strong personal boundaries. People with strong personal boundaries stay true to their beliefs, values, and feelings.

Building personal boundaries

Do you need to have stronger personal boundaries? Here are some things you can learn to do.

Build Your Confidence

- Believe in your strengths and talents.
- Respect your needs and feelings.

> People need to be happy with themselves before they can be happy with others.

Be True to Yourself

- Learn how your past experiences have affected you.
- Say "no" to behaviours that make you feel uncomfortable.
- Express your feelings and thoughts by saying "I want, I think, I need…"
- Make decisions that will help you grow to be the person you want to be.

Expect Respect from the Other Person

Healthy friendships

Friends are an important part of our lives. They help us to live more fully. They offer support when times are hard. Friends reduce stress by helping us smile and laugh more often. They lighten our day by listening, sharing interests, and providing a helping hand when we need it.

A friend is someone

who is there for you
who feels safe
you can tell secrets to
you can laugh
    and cry with
who gives hugs
who is caring and
    understanding
who jokes with you
to watch movies with

—Participants at The Learning Centre

In a healthy relationship, friends—

- are honest and open with each other
- do thoughtful things for each other
- encourage each other's hopes and dreams
- help each other
- have fun together
- resolve conflicts

Can you add to this list?
What does friendship mean to you?

Keeping friendships alive

Think of one of your close friends. It could be your partner, or someone from your community, workplace, or school. Or perhaps it is someone who lives in another city or town. Complete the chart.

	What did you do or say?	When?
Describe the last time you were honest and open with your friend.		
What was the last thoughtful thing you did for your friend?		
Describe the last time you supported your friend's hopes and dreams.		
Describe the last time you helped your friend.		
What was the last thing you and your friend enjoyed doing together?		
Describe the last conflict you resolved with your friend.		

Were you able to complete the chart? Look at the "when" column. Are the dates recent? Or is it time to focus on building your friendship?

How to build healthy friendships

FOCUS on the GOOD

Relationships get stronger when people focus on what is good about them and what is good about the people in the relationship. People can deepen their friendships when they focus on the positive. Having a deeper friendship helps keep the balance in relationships when times are hard.

- Be good to yourself.
  Do you appreciate who you are?
  Do you give yourself positive feedback?
  Are you caring and loving to yourself?
  What is something special you can do for yourself today?

  If you are good to yourself,
      you will feel good about yourself.
  If you feel good about yourself, you will find it
      easier to see the good in your friend.

- See the good in your friend.

  Sit quietly for a few minutes and think about a friend. Read the list of words below. Circle the ones that describe your friend. Are there any words you would like to add?

❖ **food for thought**

The only way to have

a friend is to be one.

—Ralph Waldo Emerson

brave	truthful	loving
thoughtful	strong	supportive
generous	creative	funny
loyal	fun	organized
cheerful	adventurous	gentle
caring	dependable	relaxed
active	warm	flexible
quiet	kind	understanding

Can you tell your friend why you appreciate them? It does not always have to be a big thing. You can say "Thank you for listening" or "Thank you for being honest with me." If you practice saying something positive you will begin to think of more things that feel special for you.

Healthy partnerships

Balance

Partners need to maintain balance in their relationship. This means partners need to share an understanding of what the relationship should look and feel like. For example, they need to find the balance between having time together and time apart.

Some couples think they need to spend all their time together. They spend every waking moment together. The "we" becomes more important than the "I" and the "you."

Other couples neglect their relationship. They live together under the same roof, but do not spend any time together. The "I' becomes more important than the "we" or the "you."

It is important for partners to share common goals, values, and interests. It is equally important for each person to meet their own personal needs. Chapter One outlined the three parts to a relationship: I, YOU, and WE. In a healthy relationship, these three parts are balanced.

I, You, and We

Here is an activity that you and your partner can do together.

(1) Each person lists seven things they like about the relationship.

   Here are some examples:

- *We talk gently to each other.*
- *We take time to have a cup of coffee together and talk about our day.*
- *We play cards in the evening.*
- *I can see my friends whenever I want.*

Share your ideas with your partner.
Together, choose five things that are important
   to both of you.
List these ideas in the "We" area of the circles.
Talk about why they are important to your relationship.

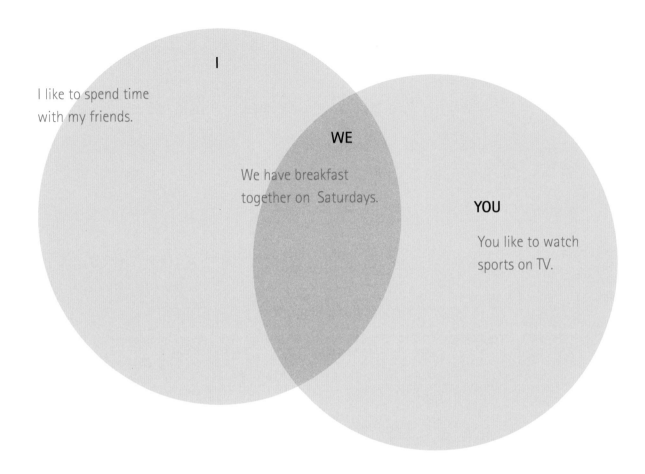

I

I like to spend time
with my friends.

WE

We have breakfast
together on Saturdays.

YOU

You like to watch
sports on TV.

(2) Each person lists seven personal needs or interests.
Share your needs and interests with your partner.
Then, each person underlines their five
most important needs and interests.
Talk about why they are important to you.
List these ideas in the "I" and "You" areas of the circles.

Post these circles in a place where you can see them every day. Make sure you pay attention to your needs as a couple and as individuals.

Summary

Relationships are not always easy. No one is born knowing how to be in relationships with other people. The best we can do is build on the good we already have and keep moving forward. •

Love is strong. It's like a rock statue of a swan.

Love is graceful as the wings of a white dove flying in a heavenly blue sky.

Love is like a hundred birds singing beautiful songs of their happiness.

Love is graceful as a ballet dancer wrapped elegantly in a bouquet of yellow lady slippers and white orchids.

Love is as strong as ten oxen pulling heavy loads over a very rough road.

Love is the strongest when the shadows and darkness come creeping in near the ending of our lifetime on this earth.

Love is a gift of life for it is of all things: happiness, sadness, sympathy and all we experience during our time on this place called earth.

—K. Steele

References and Credits

References

1   Rosenburg Self-esteem Scale.

2   Adapted from *Getting the Love You Want* by Herville Hendrix, Ph.D. Copyright © 1988 by Herville Hendrix. New York, NY. Reprinted by permission of Henry Holt and Company, LLC.

3   Adapted from Hannum, K. (2007). *Social identity: Knowing yourself, leading others.* Greensboro, N.C.: Center for Creative Leadership.

4   Moore, A. (2006). *Making it work: A workbook on conflict and communication for adult literacy learners.* Guelph, ON: Action Read.

5   Adapted from Coach U Inc. (2005). *The coach U personal and corporate coach training handbook.* New York, NY: John Wiley & Sons, Inc., p. 134.

6   Bader, E. and Pearson, P. with Schwartz, J. D. (2000). *Tell me no lies: How to stop lying to your partner—and yourself—in the four stages of marriage.* New York, NY: St. Martin's Press, pp. 50–52.

7   The Power and Control wheel was developed by the Domestic Abuse Intervention Project in Duluth, Minnesota.

Photo Credits